JOINING GOD'S GANG

BOOK ONE

JOINING GOD'S GANG

BOOK ONE

Dr. Shirley Gholston-Key

All rights reserved. No part of this book may be reproduced or utilized in any form or by any means, electronic or mechanical, including photocopying, microfilm and recording, or by any information storage and retrieval system known or to be invented, without permission in writing from the author.

ISBN 978-0-578-68588-5
© 2019 Shirley Gholston Key

JOINING GOD'S GANG

Dedicated to all youths and parents who share this book which lets youths know that they are loved <u>by</u> God and belong <u>to</u> God.

Only join God's gang!

Table of Contents

Foreword	x
Chapter 1	1
Chapter 2	5
Chapter 3	10
Chapter 4	22
Chapter 5	30
Chapter 6	40
Chapter 7	46

Your Notes	54
Your Questions	56
Tell the Author	58
Glossary	61
References	63
Share Your Opinions	65
Appendices	
Evaluators	

FOREWORD

The instruction given in the Great Commission given by the Lord Jesus Christ in Matt. 28:19-20 is: "Go, and as you go, make disciples.

What better purpose for Christ's children to be banded together for the purpose of advancing the Kingdom!

Chapter 1: Introduction

The Doubleday Roget's Thesaurus in Dictionary form cites "Gang" as a noun. Gang can be described as: a group, crew, squad, team, outfit, shift, relay, company, body, force, troop, or party.

Secondly, a gang is described as: a club, ring, band, circle, coterie, league, alliance, order, clique, mob, knot, pack, batch, and rabble.

It is readily seen that gangs have been with us from time immemorial. At its root, the Anglo-Saxon word, "gangan" i.e. gang means "to-go"

Again literally, the instruction given in the Great Commission given by the Lord Jesus Christ in Matt. 28:19-20 is: "Go, and as you go, make disciples."

In the same sense, the *Winston Dictionary, College Edition*, states that a **gang** is a group of persons banded together for a particular purpose.

What better purpose for Christ's children to be banded together for the purpose of advancing the Kingdom!

PROVERBS

- Pro = for, favor, good
- Verb = action words
- Pro + verbs = good action words

CHAPTER 2: WHY?

Why do I want to be a gang member?

"*I want to belong.*"

"*They make me feel like family.*"

"*I need a friend.*"

"*My family does not like me.*"

Those are things that new gang members say.

But…*you* do not need to say those things.

You do belong!

*Y*ou are already a gang member.

You already belong.

You belong to a family of kings and queens who love you!

The king of all kings has died for you.

The leader of the first gang, Jesus, has loved you so much he has died for you.

You owe no one anything because Jesus has paid it all for you.

Jesus has your back!

You are in Jesus' gang.

You are in his family.

You are loved!

THEN

NOW

CHAPTER 3

GANG'S LINGO: WISE SAYINGS

All gangs have their own signs, symbols, and lingo. Most gangs would like to keep their signs, symbols, and lingo a secret from others.

Unlike them, God's gang wants to share and tell everyone about the signs, symbols, and lingo of God.

God's lingo is wise sayings and are called *proverbs*.

The manual which God's gang uses is a book called the *BIBLE*.

There is a section in the BIBLE called Proverbs.

So, Proverbs is the book of wise sayings.

Your gang's rules will come from the Book of Proverbs.

In the first verse,
Proverbs1:1, you see that
Solomon, a son of David,
was given wise sayings by
God.

Proverbs are good words
and good sayings. These
good sayings are going to be
your gang's rules.

God is every one's father
or every gang member's
leader.

God places everyone in special families.

God let Solomon be born into King David's family.

And God placed Jesus into King David's family.

David was a king and a leader in God's gang.

Everybody who knows God is a king or queen.

You are a king or queen because you are tops with God!

God, the gang leader, gives advice to all gang members.

God's advice to all his gang members (his children) is found in the Bible.

That advice is called good words, good messages, or Proverbs.

These proverbs will become God gang's rules.

REMEMBER:
The proverbs of Solomon, the son of David and the king of Israel, will now become your proverbs or your gang's rules.

REMEMBER:
The good words of Jesus, the son of God and the king of the world, will guide you throughout your tasks and your life.

REMEMBER:

_____
(*write your name*)

and then say:

"I will listen to the good teachings of my parents, teachers, and all adult leaders. I am the son of the king, God. I am in a BIG gang!"

Welcome to your BIG family (BIG GANG) that loves you and teaches you.

CHAPTER 4

RULE 1: "KNOW WISDOM AND UNDERSTANDING"

In Proverbs 1:2, you are given your first rules.
You are to know wisdom and instruction and to comprehend the words of understanding.

The good and wise words of Solomon will come to you.
You are also the child of a king…God's!

God, the gang leader, will let the words come to you so that you will know how to be wise.

The words will also come to you, so that you will know how to learn to be a child of a king.

The words will also come to you so that you will know how to understand what it means to be the child of a king.

I am in God's gang.

_____
(write your name)

is smart, wise, fair, and have good behavior with everyone.

I will not be alone. I am in a BIG gang!

REMEMBER:
You are a smart member of God's gang.

You are a smart child of a king.

REMEMBER:
That lessons and wise sayings will be taught to you so that you will learn what to do and how to act like a king's child.

REMEMBER:

The way you are suppose to act as a member of God's gang will be shown to you. It will help you to know how to act as a member of God's gang and how to act as a child of God, the true gang leader.

REMEMBER:
Yes, you are in a BIG family that loves you and will help teach you!

CHAPTER 5

RULE 2: "JUSTICE, JUDGEMENT, AND EQUITY"

In Proverbs 1:3, you are told to receive the instruction of wisdom, justice, judgment, and equity.

"Wisdom is like common sense"

"We are in God's gang!"

You learn wisdom from reading your rule book and listening to what your adult leaders teach you.

As a member of God's gang, you will be asked to study, to become wise and learn how to help yourself and others.

As a member of God's gang, you will study to learn how to be fair, kind, and want the best for yourself and for others.

As a member of God's gang, you will learn how to decide right from wrong.

You will learn what is good and what is not good.

You will learn when to say "NO" because you are the child of the gang leader, God.

As a member of God's gang, you will learn to be even handed and fair with your friends.

You will learn to share the same with everyone.

You will want all your friends, brothers, and sisters, and even your enemies to join God's gang.

You will want everyone to learn about your gang leader, God- the King.

You will want everyone to know that they too, are sons and daughters of the king.

REMEMBER:
You will study your lessons to become smart and wise.

REMEMBER:
You will be fair, kind and even handed.

REMEMBER:
You will learn right from wrong, make good decisions, and teach others how to do this.

REMEMBER:
You will not be alone.

You are in a BIG gang and

You are in a big family that will love you and teach you.

CHAPTER 6

RULE 3: "BE NICE TO EVERYONE."
In Proverbs 1:4, you are told to give <u>subtilty</u> to the simple, to the youth knowledge and discretion.

"Sub-til-ty" means to help the slow minded or challenged gang members to become smart and wise.

As a member of God's
gang, you will be taught
not to be crafty, sneaky,
or slick with those not as
smart and wise as you are.

As God's gang member,
you will be shown how to
teach and help those younger
than you.

As God's gang member, you
will be taught how to teach
others to know right
from wrong for themselves.

REMEMBER:
As an older gang member, you can teach and help your younger brothers and sisters to care, to be good, and to be nice to each other.

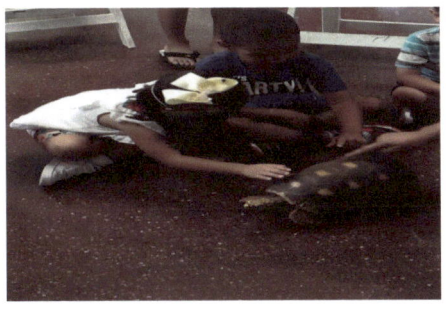

REMEMBER:
As a member of God's gang, you do not have to be "cute," "slick," or "sneaky," with your peers and non-gang members.

REMEMBER:
You will be truthful and fair like Jesus.

REMEMBER: As God's gang member, you are going to want your siblings and friends to be as smart as you are.

You are going to help them learn what you know.

You will let them know that they too can be a member of God's gang.

REMEMBER:
They are not alone. They are members of a *BIG* gang. They are members of a family that will love them and teach them, too.

CHAPTER 7

RULE 4: "LISTEN, HEAR, LEARN, AND GROW"

In Proverbs 1:5, you are taught the rule that a wise man will hear and will increase his learning. For a man of understanding shall listen to wise counsels.

For you, that rule means that as a gang member when you listen to God and do what you are taught, you will become wise.

You will hear, listen, and get *SMART* as you grow.

As a member of God's gang, your friends will be surprised at your knowledge; at your smartness and how well you think.

Finally, as a member of God's gang, your friends will notice how well you obey and follow directions and they, then will follow you!

They will follow you and obey others just as you do.

You will teach them as you go and grow.

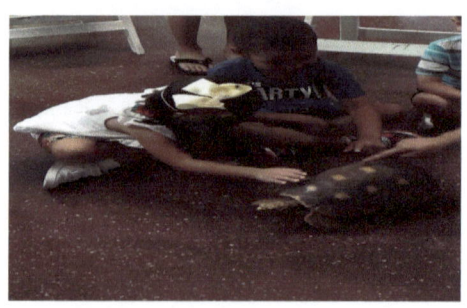

REMEMBER:

As a member of God's gang, your God will make you smarter.

REMEMBER:

As a member of God's gang, he will make you a wise leader.

REMEMBER:

As an *obedient* member of God's gang, you will have all you need, and you will know it.

But your gang leader,
God, can and will give
you some things that
    you *just want!*

REMEMBER:
You are not alone. You are a member of a BIG gang! You are a member of a family that will love and teach you.

Your Notes

What have you learned?

Show that you are becoming wiser:

Write two thoughts which you have learned.

1. _____
   _____

2. _____
   _____

???

Do you have questions?

As you read more, you might learn things that puzzle you.

Write them down.

1._____

2._____

3._____

4._____

Tell the Author…

1. What you liked about this book.

_____
_____

_____
_____

Tell the Author…

2. What you did not like about this book:

♥ _____

♥ _____

♥ _____

GLOSSARY

1. Proverbs- the wise sayings written by Solomon given to him by God.

2. King David – Solomon's father.

3. Gang member –Someone in a group being led by a leader.

4. Solomon- a son of David and the king of Israel. He wrote the wise sayings from God.

5. God – the leader of all. He made heaven, earth, all living and non-living things. He gave rules for everyone to follow.

6. Jesus- God's son whom God placed in David's family. Jesus died for all of God's gang members so that all could live and live for God only.

REFERENCES

1. Proverbs, *The Holy Bible*, King James Version.
2. Shutterstock's' pictures, (2019). www.Shutterstock.com

3. Landau, S. ,The *Doubleday Roget's Thesaurus in Dictionary Form*

4. Winston Dictionary Staff *(1946). Winston Dictionary-College Edit*

Thank you for accepting

these proverbs

and

JOINING GOD'S GANG!

Appendices

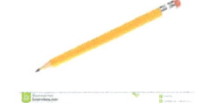

Share your opinions !

Use the wisdom which you have learned to tell the author what you think.

_____
_____
_____
_____
_____
_____

I ALSO THINK:

_____

_____

_____

What did you like about the Proverbs?

_____

_____

_____

_____

_____

What did you like about God's gang?

_____
_____
_____
_____

Mail your opinions to the Author:

Author Key
2117 Hallwood Drive
Memphis, TN 38107

or email them to

keyeducationandconsultingco@comcast.net

Other books by Dr. Shirley G. Key

Greater the Expectations... Greater the Achievement!

African American eight grade students' perceived science interest

All Children Can Learn!

About the Author

Dr. Shirley Gholston Key, an award-winning teacher and author, who started her Christian journey as a pre-schooler in Winona, Mississippi.

After leaving Mississippi as a youth and moving to Memphis, Tennessee, she united with Antioch Missionary Baptist Church and served there until after her graduation from Manassas High School. She maintained her membership with Antioch until after her graduation from Gustavus Adolphus College in St. Peter, Minnesota. She then moved to Houston, Texas with her husband, Henry Key. They united with the Sunnyside Missionary Baptist Church until their return to Memphis, Tenn. in 2002. During her tenure in Texas, Dr. Key served as Sunday School teacher, Church Missionary president, and Vacation Bible School Director while working as a public-school teacher in Fort Bend and the Houston Independent School Districts.

She also pursued her graduate work at Texas Southern University and the University of Houston while residing in Houston.

Upon her return to Memphis in 2002, she reunited with the Antioch MB Church, where she served as Sunday school teacher, Missionary president, and a Vacation Bible School teacher.

She also held a position at the University of Memphis in the College of Education as a tenured associate professor.

In 2002, she transferred her membership to St, John Baptist Church where her husband was called as the pastor. There she served as a Sunday School teacher, member of the Missionary Society, and the Director of Vacation Bible School.

Dr. Key's family, another gang for God, includes Pastor Henry Key, her husband and two children, George and Lorri. The extended family includes George's wife, Allison Davis Key and Trent Barrett, Lorri's husband, and their son, Joshua.

"YOU HAVE A PLACE RESERVED FOR YOU IN GOD'S GANG!"

These are the proverbs of King Solomon of Israel, King David's son. He wrote them to teach his people how to live and act.

How to keep from joining bad gangs:

1. Keep a high self-esteem

- Be proud of yourself

- Be proud of your work

- Do not listen to negative talk

- Compliment yourself everyday

2. Do positive things

- Volunteer to help a teacher

- Read books about people doing good things

- Join the scouts

- Join a church group

3. Exercise

- Walk in your home or your yard

- Race with a friend

- Watch exercise videos on tv

- Ride your bicycle

4. Start a Hobby

- Collect rocks

- Take pictures

- Write about things that you like or do not like

- Collect pictures of athletes

Read the Bible

5. Choose positive friends

- Get a pen pal

- Ask for a mentor from school or church
- Do not stay around person doing wrong things

- Wait for the good friend to come along

Avoid Peer Pressure!

God spoke to Solomon and Solomon spoke to our forefathers so that we could speak to you.

AS A MEMBER OF GOD'S GANG, I WILL USE THIS MANUAL.

"Kudos to Dr. Shirley G. Key for the colloquially expressed insights given to perceive Christian youths as a group of persons filled with the Spirit of God going and making disciples-as-they-go." **-Henry Key, Pastor of St. John Baptist Church (Vance).**

"Should be taught or even read to elementary students." **-Shirley Reed, Christian Educator**

"Good materials; should be shared with elementary students." **-Rev. McBride, West TN Association Moderator.**

www.ingramcontent.com/pod-product-compliance
Lightning Source LLC
Chambersburg PA
CBHW042330150426
43194CB00001B/13